Drink Me, You Must!

The Essential Star Wars cocktail book

BY - Sharon Powell

License Notes

Table of Contents

Introduction

Are you a big Star Wars fan who is planning a theme party or gathering with friends? Do you want to recreate the bar scene with Han Solo and Chewbacca in your living room? Well, grab your lightsabers and this the best Star Wars cocktail book of the Galaxy! From Yoda's Green Force to the Slug Slinger, these cocktails are fun, fresh, and full of the Force.

1. Yoda's Light Force

The force is strong with this cocktail! After 1 or 2, you will also feel as if you can move ships with your mind.

Preparation Time – 5 minutes

Servings - 1

Ingredients

- 1.5 ounces Calvados
- 1-ounce Apple cider
- 1/2-ounce simple syrup
- 1/2-ounce Fresh squeezed lemon juice
- 6 Basil leaves
- Sage leaves for garnish

Directions

Combine all ingredients except for sage leaves in a martini shaker and shake vigorously.

Strain cocktail into a martini glass and decorate with sage leaves.

2. Dark Force

When Darth Vader winds down after a long day of chasing the Rebellion, he likes to kick back and sip on a few of these delicious cocktails by using a straw, of course.

Preparation Time – 5 minutes

Servings – 1

Ingredients

- 1.5 ounces 100-proof bourbon
- 1 ounce Cynar
- 1-ounce Sweet vermouth
- 2 drops Mole bitters

Directions

Combine bourbon, Cynar, vermouth and bitters in a martini shaker and shake vigorously.

Strain liquid into a chilled glass with ice and serve.

3. Hoth Juice

Hoth was a planet of ice and snow and where the Rebel Alliance held one of their bases. This planet was also the site of the infamous scene where Solo cuts a Tauntaun and then stuffs Luke into the body of the animal to keep him warm.

Preparation Time – 5 minutes

Servings - 1

Ingredients

- 1.5 ounces rum
- 2 ounces sweetened Coconut milk
- 2 ounces Pineapple juice
- 2 ounces Fresh orange juice

Directions

Combine rum, coconut milk, pineapple juice and orange juice in a shaker and strain into a tall glass with ice.

4. The Death Star

This drink will create an explosion just the way the Death Star did to Alderaan. Sip, a young apprentice, don't gulp!

Preparation Time – 5 minutes

Servings - 1

Ingredients

- 1-ounce Jägermeister
- 1 ounce whiskey
- 1-ounce vodka
- 1-ounce Triple sec
- 2 ounces Sour mix
- 2 ounces Coke original

Directions

Mix Jägermeister, whiskey, vodka, triple sec, sour mix, and coca cola in a martini shaker and shake vigorously. Strain into a tall glass with ice.

5. Java the Hutt

This could be the inter-galactic drink of choice for Tatooine, which is ruled by the Hutts and home to the once-frozen body of Han Solo. Skywalker should have a couple of these before heading into the 'lions' den to save his friends.

Preparation Time – 5 minutes

Servings – 1

Ingredients

- 1.5 ounces vodka
- 2 ounces brewed coffee, chilled
- ½ ounce Half-and-half
- 1/4 ounce white crème de cacao liqueur
- 1/2 ounce Simple syrup
- Cinnamon sugar for garnish

Directions

Combine vodka, coffee, cream, liqueur, and syrup in a martini shaker and shake vigorously without ice.

Add crushed ice and shake for another 5 seconds.

Strain liquid into a tall glass with ice and top with a pinch of cinnamon sugar.

6. Darth Maul Cider

The deadly Sith Lord, Darth Maul would have approved of this tasty drink as a way of winding down after the long day. Just don't get too close to his double-sided saber if he drinks too much.

Preparation Time – 5 minutes

Servings – 1

Ingredients

- 8 ounces Pomegranate juice
- 4 ounces Apple cider
- 1/3 ounce Mulling spice in a mulling ball
- 1 shot whiskey

Directions

Bring juice, cider, and spice to a simmer in a saucepan on medium heat.

Simmer for 10-15 minutes and remove mulling ball.

Pour mixture into a mug and add 1 shot of whiskey.

7. Dark Side

Join the dark side…we have cool drinks! You can serve this with an edible black flower as a garnish for dramatic effect.

Preparation Time – 5 minutes

Servings – 1

Ingredients

- 1.5 ounces whiskey
- Juice from 1 lime
- 13 splashes Angostura bitters
- 1 pinch activated charcoal
- Jasmine flower for Garnish

Directions

Combine whiskey, lime bitters and charcoal in a martini shaker with ice and shake vigorously.

Strain into a chilled glass and top with a jasmine flower for garnish.

8. Qui-Gon Jinn and Tonic

The Jedi Master, who found Anakin Skywalker in a poor settlement on Tatooine, would have enjoyed one of these as he sat and chat with Skywalker's mother. Serve with a lemon rind for garnish.

Preparation Time – 5 minutes

Servings – 1

Ingredients

- 2 ounces tonic water
- 2 ounces gin
- 6 ounces cold-brew coffee
- Lemon rind for garnish

Directions

Fill a highball glass with ice and pour tonic in the glass.

In a separate glass, combine gin and coffee. Stir well.

Pour coffee mixture over the tonic in the highball glass.

Press oil out of the lemon rind and add to the liquid.

9. Kylo Rye

Out of all the characters in the Star Wars epic, Kylo Ren is one of the most tragic. The tortured son of Leia and Han could use a good drink.

Preparation Time – 5 minutes

Servings – 1

Ingredients

- 2 ounces rye whiskey
- 0.25 ounces fresh-squeezed lime juice
- Club soda
- Lime twist to garnish

Directions

Add ice to a Collins glass and pour whiskey and juice over the ice.

Add club soda to fill the glass and a lime twist as garnish.

10. Flying Solo

I like to serve this drink with a small blue glowstick for dramatic effect. This cocktail is delicious and will help pass the time while hiding from your favourite bounty hunter.

Preparation Time – 5 minutes

Servings – 1

Ingredients

- 1.5 ounces tequila
- ½ ounce Agave nectar
- ½ ounce freshly squeezed lemon juice
- 1-ounce White Zinfandel

Directions

Combine the first three ingredients in a martini shaker with ice and strain into a glass filled with ice cubes.

Pour zinfandel to fill the glass and serve with a glowstick.

11. Surly Sarlacc

If you remember Jabba's Sarlacc pit, you will recall the creature was not cute and cuddly. This drink has a lovely tangy taste that is cool and refreshing when staring down the jaws of a massive beast.

Preparation Time – 5 minutes

Servings – 1

Ingredients

- 4 ounces cold water
- 1 ½ ounces Frozen Limeade from Concentrate
- 1-ounce mango syrup
- ½ ounce raspberry syrup
- 1-ounce Botanical Grapefruit and Rose Vodka

Directions

Stir limeade and water until combined in a container. Add the rest of the **Ingredients** and stir well.

Pour into a glass with ice.

12. Bothan's cocktail

While it is a common misconception that the Bothan's were the ones who provided the Rebellion with the plans to the Death Star, that is, in fact, untrue. The Bothan's did divulge the whereabouts of the Death Star and when the Emperor would visit, but they never produced any plans.

Preparation Time – 5 minutes

Servings - 1

Ingredients

- 1-ounce silver tequila
- 3 ounces club soda
- 1 lime cut in wedges
- ice

Directions

Add ice to a 10-ounce glass. Pour in tequila and juice from ½ lime.

Fill the rest of the glass with club soda.

Garnish with a lime wedge.

13. Valley of the Dark Lords

The Dark Lords enjoy a drink or two when they get together to trade leadership tips and anecdotes. Steer clear after they have had one or two of them as you may find yourself being lifted by an invisible hand.

Preparation Time – 5 minutes

Servings – 1

Ingredients

- 1 oz mezcal
- 0.75 oz chile liqueur
- 0.75 oz cherry liqueur
- 0.75 oz freshly squeezed orange juice
- 1 pinch ground Turmeric
- 1 tsp Chia seeds

Directions

Combine mezcal, chile and cherry liqueur and orange juice in a martini shaker and shake vigorously.

Strain liquid into a chilled glass and serve.

14. Yoda drink

I love the way this drink looks like when you serve it to your guests. Enjoy with some pickled beans or a splash of tabasco sauce.

Preparation Time – 5 minutes

Servings – 1

Ingredients

- 1 Jalapeño pepper, cut in half
- 1 jalapeno pepper, sliced
- 1-ounce Honey syrup (1/2-ounce honey mixed with ½ ounce water)
- 1/2-ounce Matcha concentrate
- 0.75 ounces freshly squeezed lime juice
- 1-ounce mezcal
- 1-ounce coco liqueur
- 4 splashes Orange flower water

Directions

Muddle 3 slices of jalapeno with honey water, lime juice and Matcha concentrate in a martini shaker.

Add the rest of the ingredients except for halved jalapeno and shake well.

Strain mixture into a glass with ice and cut the halved jalapenos with a slit to test them on the sides of the glass.

15. Mo Greedo

Make a couple of these cocktails to honor the green-skinned bounty hunter from the first Star Wars movie ever made. Just don't have too many or you might end up shooting second.

Preparation Time – 5 minutes

Servings – 1

Ingredients

- 2 ounces rum
- 1 ounce freshly squeezed lime juice
- 1-ounce Creme de Menthe
- 1/3-ounce sugar
- Soda water

Directions

Muddle sugar and lime juice in a shaker and pour into a glass.

Add ice and pour in rum and Crème de Menthe.

Fill the rest of the glass with soda water and stir.

Use a lime slice to garnish the glass and serve.

16. Tatooine Sunrise

Double the sun means double the spectacular sunrise. Serve this with some maraschino cherries on top for garnish.

Preparation Time – 5 minutes

Servings – 1

Ingredients

- 1 ounce tequila
- 2 ounces orange juice
- 2 maraschino cherries
- Grenadine syrup

Directions

Place glass into the freezer to chill and add tequila and orange juice. Slowly add grenadine by the spoonful to create a pool at the bottom of the glass. Garnish with cherries and enjoy.

17. Darth Collins

Join the Dark Side of the Force with the evil twin of Tom Collins. They still have their perks.

Preparation Time – 5 minutes

Servings – 1

Ingredients

- 1-ounce vodka
- 1-ounce lemon juice
- Soda water
- 1 teaspoon simple syrup

Directions

Add all vodka, lemon juice and simple syrup to a martini shaker and pour into a glass with ice. Top up with soda water and enjoy.

18. ATAT Knees

Once you have a few of these, you will feel weak in the knees like the All Terrain Armored Transport.

Preparation Time – 5 minutes

Servings – 1

Ingredients

- 1.5 ounces gin
- 1-ounce lemon juice
- 1-ounce organic honey

Directions

Combine gin, lemon juice and honey in a martini shaker with ice and strain into a glass.

19. Dark N' Stormy

When the Sith Lords get together to relax, kick back and have a few drinks, this is one of their favourites. The Dark side is always stormy but, oh, so delicious.

Preparation Time – 5 minutes

Servings – 1

Ingredient

- ½ ounce simple syrup
- 3 ounces ginger beer
- ½ ounce lime juice
- 1-ounce Goslings dark rum

Directions

Add ice to the glass and pour dark and ginger beer into the glass. Add lime juice and simple syrup and stir gently. Garnish with a lime wedge.

20. Jinn and Tonic II

This simple gin and tonic cocktail will have your Midichlorians rising and your lightsaber glowing. Try it with a wedge of lime or lemon.

Preparation Time – 5 minutes

Servings – 1

Ingredients

- 1 ounce gin
- 2 ounces tonic water
- Lime

Directions

Pour gin and tonic water into a glass with ice and garnish with a lemon wedge.

21. Hot Tauntaun

After a cold day curled up in a Tauntaun to keep warm, you will need one of these cocktails. Warm-up your belly and drink away those terrible memories with a Hot Tauntaun.

Preparation Time – 5 minutes

Servings – 1

Ingredients

- 1 ounce whiskey
- 2 ounces hot water
- 1/3-ounce dark sugar
- 1/3 ounce freshly squeezed lemon juice
- 1 Cinnamon stick
- 1 lemon wedge

Directions

Add whiskey, water, dark sugar and lemon juice to a mug or a glass.

Add cinnamon stick and lemon wedge for garnish.

22. Admiral Ackbar's Sazerac

The Admiral may think that this drink might be a trap, but it is, in fact, the best way to end a day of fending off Vader. Unfortunately, Ackbar was not successful in that, but you can have a couple of these in his memory.

Preparation Time – 5 minutes

Servings – 1

Ingredients

- 1 ¼ ounces rye whiskey
- ½ ounces absinthe
- 3 splashes Peychaud's Bitters
- 1 cube of white sugar
- water
- Lemon peel for garnish

Directions

Pour absinthe into a chilled glass and roll it around to coat the bottom and sides. Add crushed ice and stir.

In another glass, add bitters, white sugar cube and 2-3 drops of water and stir.

Add whiskey to the bitters and ice and stir.

Remove ice and absinthe from the first glass and strain whiskey mixture into the glass.

Add a lemon peel for garnish.

23. Finn Fizz

That tricky Finn realizes that he has true feelings for the Resistance, especially Rey. While he is nursing this drink, he is feeling this conflict within.

Preparation Time – 5 minutes

Servings – 1

Ingredients

- 1 ounce vodka
- ½ ounce freshly squeezed lemon juice
- ½ ounce blue curacao
- 1 teaspoon simple syrup
- Soda water

Directions

Combine all ingredients except for soda water in a tall glass with ice. Fill the top with soda water and garnish with a lemon wedge.

24. Rise of Skywalker

The movie moment where Skywalker realizes his true purpose in the universe with Rey is the perfect moment to sip on this cocktail. Serve with an apple wedge as garnish.

Preparation Time – 5 minutes

Servings – 1

Ingredients

- 2 ounces brandy
- 1-ounce apple brandy
- 1-ounce vermouth

Directions

Combine all ingredients in a martini shaker and strain into a cocktail glass.

25. Fuzzy Tauntaun

It is hard to remember the moment where Solo cuts open a Tauntaun to save his friend, Luke. This drink will remind you that there is a good side to the Tauntaun, not just its innards.

Preparation Time – 5 minutes

Servings – 1

Ingredients

- 6 ounces Simply Orange Juice
- 1 ½ ounces Peach Vodka
- ½ ounces Pure Cane Syrup
- ½ ounce Peach Schnapps

Directions

Combine orange juice, vodka, cane syrup and peach schnapps in a shake and shake well.
Pour into a glass with ice and enjoy.

26. Jedi Mind Trick

This is the drink you are looking for! When you sip on one or three of these delicious concoctions, you will also forget about the droids you were sent to find.

Preparation Time – 5 minutes

Servings – 1

Ingredients

- 1 ½ ounces Grapefruit and Rose Vodka
- 1-ounce white grape juice
- 1-ounce Velvet Falernum
- 1 tsp Blue Curacao
- 1 tsp lime juice
- 1 splash grapefruit bitters

Directions

Combine vodka, grape juice, falernum, blue curacao, lime juice and bitters in a martini shaker and shake well.

Pour into a glass with ice and enjoy.

27. The Outer Rim

Nothing is as stunning as the view from the Millennium Falcon when traversing the outer rim. It is even more beautiful with a few of these cocktails in your system.

Preparation Time – 5 minutes

Servings – 1

Ingredients

- 2 ounces tequila
- 1 ounce freshly squeezed lime juice
- 3/4-ounce orange liqueur
- 1 tsp granulated sugar
- black salt
- frozen exotic fruit blend

Directions

Place 2 ounces of exotic fruit blend in a blender and puree.

Mix tequila, lime juice, orange liqueur and sugar in a martini shaker and shake well.

Wet rim with lime and place in black salt.

Pour tequila mixture into a glass and top with the pureed fruit blend.

28. T-162 Skyhopper

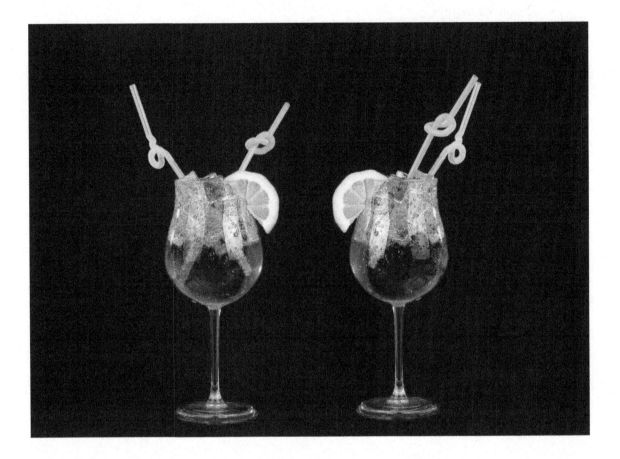

Luke owned a Skyhopper on Tatooine when he was living there with his aunt and uncle. This is the vehicle that most young pilots practice until they graduate.

Preparation Time – 5 minutes

Servings – 1

Ingredients

- 1.5 ounces heavy whipping cream
- 1.5 ounces kiwi syrup
- ¾ ounce green melon liqueur
- 1.5 ounces vodka

Directions

Mix all ingredients in a martini shaker with ice and strain into a tall glass with ice.

Garnish with a kiwi slice.

29. Slug Slinger

The Dagobah slug is a drink that was served at Oga's Cantina, which was supposed to possess medicinal purposes. It is safe for human consumption, but I wouldn't have many of them at Oga's.

Preparation Time – 5 minutes

Servings – 1

Ingredients

- 3 ounces reposado tequila
- 8 ounces grapefruit juice
- 2 ounces simple syrup
- 2 ounces orange juice
- ¼ ounce lime juice
- ¼ ounce blue curacao
- 1 tsp citrus bitters
- 2 sprigs rosemary

Directions

Fill a martini shaker with ice and combine all ingredients in the shaker. Shake well

Strain mixture into two cocktail glasses with ice and top with a sprig of rosemary.

30. Jet Juice

One of the Star Wars-themed drinks at Oga's Cantina in California is the delicious Jet Juice that will fuel your inner jets and have you running on fumes. Serve this drink with a lemon wedge for garnish.

Preparation Time – 5 minutes

Servings – 1

Ingredients

- 1-ounce mild bourbon
- 2 ounces Acai Liqueur
- 2 ounces Ancho Reyes Chili Liqueur
- 2 ounces Lemon Juice
- 2 ounces White Grape Juice

Directions

Mix all ingredients in a martini shaker and strain into a glass with ice. Serve and enjoy!

Conclusion

From Java the Hutt to the Surly Sarlacc, this cocktail recipe book has something even the most discerning Sith Lord can enjoy. The ingredients can be found in any liquor store and the directions are simple and straightforward. Don't forget to share with your family and friends. Enjoy!

About the Author

As a child, spending time in the kitchen excited Sharon. She particularly enjoyed her family ritual of cooking together during the weekends, but she didn't think that would be her path. Actually, at the time, she thought she could only be a chef or own a restaurant and wasn't sure if she could pull it off.

She spent most of her mid-20s in a cubicle at an advertising agency where she worked as a copywriter. At every chance she got, she let herself dream and pen down cooking ideas, which she would experiment with and try to create whenever she got the chance.

She wanted more as her yearning for food cultures grew. After a eureka moment, she figured out that she didn't have to be a chef or own a restaurant before she did what had always been a part of her. She did some research and found out a catering school where she earned a diploma.

Deciding to write as much as she can about food, she took up part-time editor roles at food blogs and also ghostwrote a couple of cookbooks before she branched out to do her thing.

She resigned her job and turned her home, which she shared with her fiancé to her office. A decade later, she shares it with her husband, their two kids, and a dog, and she is still writing about food.

Author's Afterthoughts

Perhaps, one of the greatest fears a writer has is to be the author of a book no one reads. This fear lingers for so long that it takes a lot to shake it off – if you shake it off. So, you must know how thankful I am to you, my reader that you went for this book and read it. Believe me, it is a dream come true.

We have connected with this book, and I would like for us to stay connected. I would like to hear your thoughts about the book, and I am sure there others who are waiting for comments such as yours to decide if this book is the right fit for them. If you enjoyed reading this book and learned something from it, (I hope you did) I would like to ask you to leave a review. I hope that it is not too much trouble.

My sincerest thanks,

Sharon Powell

Made in the USA
Las Vegas, NV
01 March 2022

44793319R00039